CLAIM the Life

Semester 1

Promise

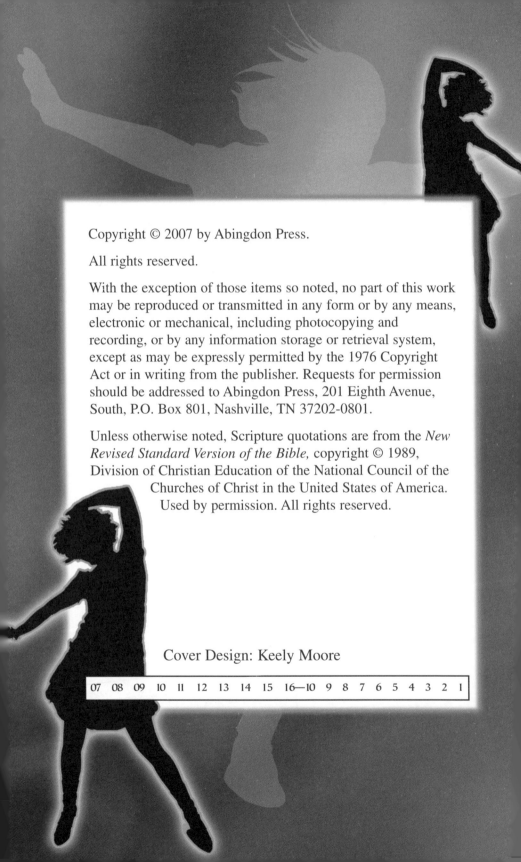

Cover Design: Keely Moore

07 08 09 10 11 12 13 14 15 16—10 9 8 7 6 5 4 3 2 1

Contents

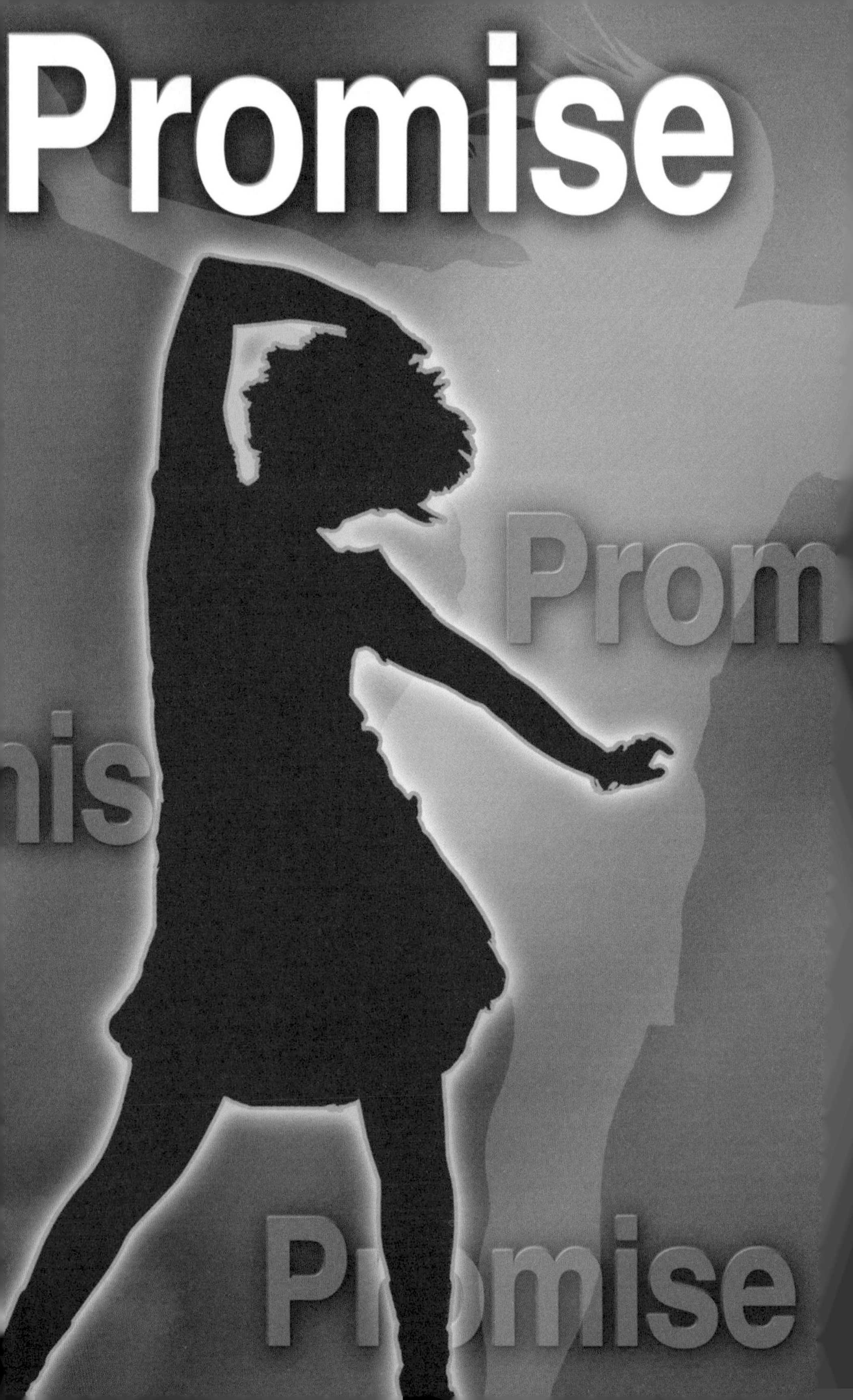
Promise
Prom
nis
Promise

Promise

> **promise** (PRAH-miss) *v.* To assure someone that one will do something or that something will happen.
> **promise** *n.* A statement or assurance that one will do something or that something will happen.

When God made a promise to Abraham, because [God] had no one greater by whom to swear, [God] swore by [God's own] self, saying, "I will surely bless you and multiply you." And thus Abraham, having patiently endured, obtained the promise. Human beings, of course, swear by someone greater than themselves, and an oath given as confirmation puts an end to all dispute. In the same way, when God desired to show even more clearly to the heirs of the promise the unchangeable character of [God's] purpose, [God] guaranteed it by an oath, so that through two unchangeable things, in which it is impossible that God would prove false, we who have taken refuge might be strongly encouraged to seize the hope set before us.

Let us hold fast to the confession of our hope without wavering, for [God] who has promised is faithful.

—Hebrews 6:13-18; 10:23

iT HAPPENS

These fictional stories are based on real-life events.

My brother died last week. We thought he had finally kicked his habit after all these years of him in and out of treatment. In fact, he told us he was working hard at being clean. We don't know exactly what happened, because he seemed so happy lately. All we know is that he didn't show up for work. A friend came to the house to pick him up and found him on the bedroom floor. I know that God promised to love us, but does God still care about my brother? What about us?

What I think ...

I just came back from a work camp where 300 youth helped renovate more than fifty homes in five days. It was an awesome experience. I made lots of friends. I learned a lot, and I discovered that I can make a difference. On our last night together, we sang a song by Casting Crowns called "Who Am I?" It really touched me to know that God cares about me personally and promises to be with me wherever I am. Now I am wondering: *Was it all real? I felt God's promises come alive last week, but how will this experience make any difference when I go back to school?*

What I think ...

My "friends" call me—well, I won't tell you what they call me. Let's just say that I can mess up almost any situation. In fact, as a joke, they once put me in a garbage can and took my picture. Sometimes it seems as if everyone but me has it all together. I keep wondering how I fit in this world. I talked with my youth leader about it, and she said that you see a rainbow only in the middle of a storm. What does that mean?

What I think ...

God Promises

"I have set my bow in the clouds, and it shall be a sign of the covenant between me and the earth."

—Genesis 9:13

"Know that I am with you and will keep you wherever you go."

—Genesis 28:15a

"They will not hurt or destroy on all my holy mountain, for the earth will be full of the knowledge of the Lord as the waters cover the sea."

—Isaiah 11:9

"I have called you by name, you are mine."

—Isaiah 43:1b

I will be their God, and they shall be my people.

—Jeremiah 31:33b

"Come to me, all you that are weary and are carrying heavy burdens, and I will give you rest."

—Matthew 11:28

"Remember, I am with you always, to the end of the age."

—Matthew 28:20b

"To the thirsty I will give water as a gift from the spring of the water of life. Those who conquer will inherit these things, and I will be their God and they will be my children."

—Revelation 21:6b-7

Which promise is the most important to you? Why?

Which promise is the least important? Why?

What do these promises tell us about God?

What do these promises tell us about our relationship to God?

Which promise could make the most difference to you in the week ahead? How might it make a difference?

Let us hold fast to the confession of our hope without wavering, for [God] who has promised is faithful.

(Hebrews 10:23)

What does this Scripture tell you about God?

What does this Scripture tell you about your relationship with God?

A Message Board on Promise Rings

To protect anonymity, the following is a adaptation of a thread found on the Internet:

Post #1 @ 07-13-07, 05:26 P.M.   Reply

Have you ever been given a promise ring?

Post #2 @ 07-13-07, 05:58 P.M.   Reply

My boyfriend told me he would give me a promise ring this weekend.
I can't wait!

Post #3 @ 07-13-07, 06:12 P.M.   Reply

I have a promise ring. The problem is that we broke up two months ago.
But that's a LOOOONG story.

Post #4 @ 07-13-07, 07:15 P.M.   Reply

My best friend got one from her bf. I am sooo jealous!

Post #5 @ 07-13-07, 08:53 P.M.   Reply

I have one. We're planning to get married in a couple of years.

Post your response here:

Relationship

relationship (reh-LAY-shuhn-ship) *n.* The way in which two or more beings are connected or behave toward one another.

concentric circles

- In the white circle, write words or phrases that describe who you are.
- In the blue circle, write words or phrases that define how your friends would describe you.
- In the gold circle, write words or phrases that describe how other people perceive you—what they think they know about you or what you think they see in you. Keep in mind that these ideas may be totally wrong or off base.

Close By Me

✳ On a date...how would you feel having Jesus sitting next to you and your date at the movie theater? Would his presence make a difference in the kinds of movies you watch? Would it change the way you and your date talk or behave toward each other?

✳ Playing football or another sport...how might your game be different if Jesus were playing on the opposing team? Would it affect the language you use? Would it change the way you handle a win? What about a loss?

✳ Friday nights . . . would you feel comfortable taking Jesus with you to a party? How might your evening be different if you knew that Jesus were there watching everything you did? Would God be proud of the way you spend your time?

Having an intimate relationship with God means carrying Christ with you through every day and every activity. Are you willing to be that close? Are you willing to get to know God in a close and personal way?

What's in a Name?

In the passage found in Romans 8:12-17, we are invited to call God by the name of Abba. *Abba* is an Aramaic word meaning "father." Two other passages in the New Testament use Abba.

Look up the following verses and paraphrase them:

Mark 14:36 _____

_____

Galatians 4:6 _____

_____

What are some other names for God?

_____   _____

_____   _____

_____   _____

Why do you think God invites us to call God this special name?

_____

_____

_____

_____

What Will You Inherit?

According to **Romans 8:14-17,** "All who are led by the Sprit of God are children of God, . . . and joint heirs with Jesus Christ." An heir is someone whose relationship—either by family ties or by choice—entitles him or her to receive something that is passed on from someone else. Solve this crossword puzzle to see some of what you will gain as a child of God and co-heir with Jesus Christ.

ACROSS

2. "God, from whom all _____ flow"
4. A "daddy" name we can call God
6. What you get when you're born again
7. How long we'll spend in heaven
8. Greater than faith and hope

DOWN

1. What we sometimes go through with Christ
3. Free gift
4. God's claiming us as God's children
5. What Jesus left his disciples

Belonging

belonging (beh-LAHNG-eeng) *n.* Fitting in a certain place or environment.

For whoever was called in the Lord as a slave is a freed person belonging to the Lord, just as whoever was free when called is a slave of Christ. You were bought with a price; do not become slaves of human masters. In whatever condition you were called, brothers and sisters, there remain with God.

–1 Corinthians 7:22-24

[To the slaves who are believers] I'm simply trying to point out that under your new Master you're going to experience a marvelous freedom you would never have dreamed of. On the other hand, if you were free when Christ called you, you'll experience a delightful "enslavement to God" you would never have dreamed of. All of you, slave and free both, were once held hostage in a sinful society. Then a huge sum was paid out for your ransom. So please don't, out of old habit, slip back into being or doing what everyone else tells you. Friends, stay where you were called to be. God is there.

—1 Corinthians 7:22-24 (Message)

What's It Worth?

Suppose that the items below could be purchased with money and that you have been given $500,000 to spend at this auction.

You need to decide how much money you would be willing to pay for each item listed below. You must use all of the $500,000. These items will go to the highest bidder. Once an amount of money has been bid, it cannot be transferred to another item.

Use this page to decide which items to bid on and how much you want to bid.

_____	Honesty	_____	Happiness
_____	Achievement	_____	Knowledge
_____	Justice	_____	Recognition
_____	Wealth	_____	Religion
_____	Love	_____	Pleasure
_____	Power	_____	Freedom
_____	Peace	_____	Wisdom
_____	Joy	_____	Altruism
_____	Health	_____	Discipline
_____	Beauty	_____	Patience

What's it worth to me?

What do you think? Write your reflections here:

GOD DOESN'T CARE

God doesn't care

whether you are rich or poor,

whether you are school smart or smart
in other ways,

whether you've received awards or
recognition for your talents and skills,
or your talents and skill are yet to be
discovered or developed.

God doesn't care

if you're cute or handsome,

whether you've been labeled "a good kid"
or something else.

External stuff doesn't define you. God
knows the real you.

God loves you as you are.

God gives you a place of belonging—
in God's heart!

Judgment

> **judgment** (JUHJ-mehnt) *n.* An opinion, formed after consideration, about something or someone.

You Be the Judge

Type of object: _____

Circle the number that best describes the item you are scoring.

	Worst		Best
Solidness of construction	1 2 3 4 5 6	7	8 9 10
Level of detail	1 2 3 4 5	6 7	8 9 10
Color choices	1 2 3 4 5 6 7 8 9 10		
Aesthetic appeal	1 2 3 4 5 6 7 8 9 10		
Team effort	1 2 3 4 5 6 7 8 9 10		
Length of building time	1 2 3 4 5 6 7 8 9 10		
Ability to carry out intended function			
(such as rolling or floating)	1 2 3 4 5 6 7 8 9 10		

Overall score: _____

It's God We Are Answerable To

It's *God* we are answerable to—all the way from life to death and everything in between—not one another....

...So where does that leave you when you criticize a brother? And where does that leave you when you condescend to a sister? I'd say it leaves you looking pretty silly—or worse. Eventually, we're all going to end up kneeling side by side in the place of judgment, facing God. Your critical and condescending ways aren't going to improve your position there one bit. Read it for yourself in Scripture:

"As I live and breathe," God says,
"every knee will bow before me;
Every tongue will tell the honest truth
that I and only I am God."

So tend to your knitting. You've got your hands full just taking care of your own life before God.

—Romans 14:8, 10-12 (*Message*)

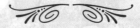

When we look at others, can we ever see the whole picture?

What's the difference between God's perspective
and ours? Will any judgments we make be
completely accurate?

What does that answer say about
our judging others?

How does knowing that God will judge
all of us make you feel?

How will that knowledge affect how you live?

"Do not judge, and you will not be judged. Do not condemn, and you will not be condemned. Forgive, and you will be forgiven."

— Luke 6:37 (NIV)

For God will bring every deed into judgment, including every hidden thing, whether it is good or evil.

—Ecclesiastes 12:14 (NIV)

For we must all appear before the judgment seat of Christ, that each one may receive what is due him (or her) for the things done while in the body, whether good or bad.

—2 Corinthians 5:10 (NIV)

Then the righteous will shine like the sun
in the kingdom of their Father. Let anyone
with ears listen!

—Matthew 13:43 (NRSV)

When through fiery trials
        your pathway shall lie,
    my grace, all sufficient,
            shall be your supply;

the flame shall not hurt you;
        I only design
    your dross to consume,
            and your gold to refine.

—from the hymn "How Firm a Foundation"

Blessing

> **blessing** (BLEH-seeng) *n.* 1. God's protection and favor. 2. A prayer asking for such protection and favor. 3. A good thing for which one is grateful.

TIME CAPSULE

1. A blessing I received without ever asking for it:

2. A blessing I received from an unlikely person or situation:

3. A blessing that at the time felt like bad news but turned out to be a blessing:

What was difficult, freeing, surprising, or new about this exercise?

Claim the Life: Promise, Semester

Thoughts on Blessings

Blessings are about life. God longs for us to choose life always, to receive God's blessings and to live in ways that allow us to recognize when we've been blessed.

God blesses humanity again and again, sometimes using God's mysterious, divine ways to shower people with surprising blessings—such as when Sarah and Abraham were promised they would be parents! God uses parents to bless people, as when Isaac blessed his sons, Jacob and Esau. More often than not, God uses our actions of faithfulness to bless us. God chooses to bless us in so many ways that we can't name them all.

The funny thing about blessings is that it can take us a while to figure out that we've been blessed.

Whatever the case, God's blessings require a response from us. Although the details may vary, a faithful response is always rooted in actions of faith, trust, and obedience. Responding faithfully deepens the blessing we receive.

The funny thing about blessings is that it can take us a while to figure out that we've been blessed. Some blessings are obvious, such as food, water, shelter, and family to care for us. We didn't do anything to deserve being born in a country where these things are readily available, but we can easily forget that such basic things are blessings because most of us have always had them. Displaced people living through war in Darfur, Sudan, or Iraq would probably readily recognize food, water, and shelter as blessings. Can you think of some other undeserved blessings we have that we tend to forget?

Make a list of ways God has blessed you, regardless of anything you've done to receive these gifts.

Now make a list of specific people who know who could use your prayers for specific blessings.

The Word on Blessings

When the LORD your God has brought you into the land that [God] swore to your ancestors, to Abraham, to Isaac, and to Jacob, to give you—a land with fine, large cities that you did not build, houses filled with all sorts of goods that you did not fill, hewn cisterns that you did not hew, vineyards and olive groves that you did not plant—and when you have eaten your fill, take care that you do not forget the LORD, who brought you out of the land of Egypt, out of the house of slavery.

(Deuteronomy 6:10-12)

"I gave you a land on which you had not labored, and towns that you had not built. . . . Now therefore revere the Lord, and serve [God] in sincerity and in faithfulness."

(Joshua 24:13-14)

- **What do these passages teach us about God's blessings and the part we play?**

The Blessed Sermon

Spectator 1: I think it was, "Blessed are the cheesemakers."

Mrs. Gregory: Aha, what's so special about the cheesemakers?

Gregory: Well, obviously it's not meant to be taken literally; it refers to any manufacturers of dairy products.

This dialogue is from the Monthy Python movie *The Life of Brian*. The comedy deals with what would happen if the three wise men chose the wrong baby to worship when Jesus was born. The well-known quotation above is taken from the scene where people are listening to Jesus say the Beatitudes, part of the Sermon on the Mount. The crowd hears what they want to hear and not the reality and wisdom that Christ offers. The real script comes from **Matthew 5:3-12** and describes the blessings God offers people.

Reflections:

"**BLESSED** ARE THE POOR IN SPIRIT, FOR THEIRS IS THE KINGDOM OF HEAVEN.

"**BLESSED** ARE THOSE WHO MOURN, FOR THEY WILL BE COMFORTED.

"**BLESSED** ARE THE MEEK, FOR THEY WILL INHERIT THE EARTH.

"**BLESSED** ARE THOSE WHO HUNGER AND THIRST FOR RIGHTEOUSNESS, FOR THEY WILL BE FILLED.

"**BLESSED** ARE THE MERCIFUL, FOR THEY WILL RECEIVE MERCY.

"**BLESSED** ARE THE PURE IN HEART, FOR THEY WILL SEE GOD.

"**BLESSED** ARE THE PEACEMAKERS, FOR THEY WILL BE CALLED CHILDREN OF GOD. BLESSED ARE THOSE WHO ARE PERSECUTED FOR RIGHTEOUSNESS' SAKE, FOR THEIRS IS THE KINGDOM OF HEAVEN.

"**BLESSED** ARE YOU WHEN PEOPLE REVILE YOU AND PERSECUTE YOU AND UTTER ALL KINDS OF EVIL AGAINST YOU FALSELY ON MY ACCOUNT. REJOICE AND BE GLAD, FOR YOUR REWARD IS GREAT IN HEAVEN, FOR IN THE SAME WAY THEY PERSECUTED THE PROPHETS WHO WERE BEFORE YOU."

MATTHEW 5:3-12

• What does Jesus' sermon teach us about blessings?

• According to this passage, what characteristics make someone blessed?

- How is this description different from what we think being blessed means?

- What is difficult to understand about this notion of blessings?

- Do you think Abraham would be able to relate to any of these aspects of what being blessed means? Explain your answer.

Steadfast Love

steadfast (STEHD-fast) *adj.* Firm, unwavering.

love (luhv) *n.* 1. An intense feeling of deep fondness or affection. 2. A great pleasure and interest in something.

abound (uh-BOUND) *v.* To occur or exist in great numbers or amounts.

infinite (IN-fih-nit) *adj.* 1. Unbounded or unlimited; perfect. 2. Impossible to measure.

"The LORD, the LORD,
a God merciful and gracious, slow to anger,
and abounding in steadfast love and faithfulness,
keeping steadfast love for the thousandth generation."
(Exodus 34:6b-7a)

The steadfast love of the LORD never ceases,
[God's] mercies never come to an end;
they are new every morning;
great is your faithfulness.
(Lamentations 3:22-23)

INTERVIEW THE EXPERTS

Use the space below to make notes about the "expert" you are assigned.

- What's your name?

- Where are you from?

- What do you do for a living?

- What's a typical day in your life like?

- Do you believe that God's steadfast love is real? Why, or why not? (Support your opinion with facts, either from your culture or the Bible.)

- What do you think will be your opponents' biggest argument to tear down your position on God's steadfast love? What is your response?

- Since you have a national platform on this talk show, what message would you most like to tell the world about God's steadfast love?

Discover Infinity

Station 1: You will see a large figure. Draw it yourself and describe it below. Note anything else you know about this figure.

Station 2: Stand between the two mirrors, and look at your reflection. How many of you do you see? Note any other thoughts you have about seeing your reflection this way.

Station 3: Take the marker and draw the longest line possible on the strip of paper. How long is the line? What would you need to make it longer? Note any other thoughts you have about drawing the line.

• What is infinity?

What do the figure, mirrors, and line have to do with the concept of infinity?

RESPOND TO GOD'S PROMISE

Write a journal entry below describing how you understand the nature of God's steadfast love. Can you easily believe that God's love goes on forever, or do you find that concept difficult? Why? How readily can you accept the nature of God's abounding love?

Thinking about the concept of infinity and reading and hearing the Scripture, how, would you say, has God demonstrated steadfast love in your life?

Emmanuel

Emmanuel (eh-MAN-yoo-uhl) *n.* A name meaning "God is with us" that the prophet Isaiah gave to Jesus as the deliverer of Judah

"Look, the virgin shall conceive and bear a son, and they shall name him Emmanuel."
—Matthew 1:23

THE WORD ON GOD'S PRESENCE

- Jesus was born in Bethlehem of Judea.
    —Matthew 2:1

(The word *Bethlehem* means "house of bread.")

- Jesus said to them, "I am the bread of life. Whoever comes to me will never be hungry, and whoever believes in me will never be thirsty."
    —John 6:35

- Again Jesus spoke to them, saying, "I am the light of the world. Whoever follows me will never walk in darkness but will have the light of life."
    —John 8:12

- "You are the light of the world.... Let your light shine before others, so that they may see your good works and give glory to your Father in heaven."
    —Matthew 5:14a, 16

- "And I tell you, you are Peter, and on this rock I will build my church, and the gates of Hades will not prevail against it. I will give you the keys of the kingdom of heaven, and whatever you bind on earth will be bound in heaven, and whatever you loose on earth will be loosed in heaven."
    —Matthew 16:18-19

(This passage relates to the authority of God's church and the role of church leaders to represent Christ.)

Claim the Life: Promise, Semester

- " 'For I was hungry and you gave me food, I was thirsty and you gave me something to drink, I was a stranger and you welcomed me, I was naked and you gave me clothing, I was sick and you took care of me, I was in prison and you visited me.' "

—Matthew 25:35-36

Reflections:

God-Bearer

Did you know that in the history of the church, Mary's pregnancy and childbirth had an official word? It is *theotokos*, and the original Greek means "God-Bearer."

However, not everyone in the early church could agree to think of Mary as having given birth to God. Some people thought the term confused the identity of Mary too much, suggesting she was more than human. Others felt it highlighted her special role in God's salvation of humanity. Nowadays the most popular definition of *theotokos* is "Mother of God"; the term is mostly used in the Eastern Orthodox Church and the Catholic Church.

The idea of being a God-bearer has importance for us. As Christian disciples, we are called to go out into the world and share the gospel; we are essentially being asked to be God-bearers, to carry Christ in our words and our actions. As we go, we know that God is with us.

What's in a Name?

When God came to earth through Jesus Christ, God picked a name for him that would reveal something intimate and significant about God's identity and feelings about us.

The prophet Isaiah didn't say, "Look, the virgin shall conceive and bear a son; and they shall call him Nigel, or Charley even — that has a nice ring." The Jews of Mary's generation knew that names were important. People named they children in ways that described God's actions, the people's longings for God, or their feelings toward God.

Here are some names surrounding the birth of Christ:

Messiah: anointed one

Jesus: God will save

Mary: wished-for child

Joseph: God will increase

David: friend, beloved

Emmanuel: God is with us
        (Matthew 1:18-25)

Zechariah: God remembers

Aaron: exalted

Elizabeth: oath of God

John: God is gracious

Gabriel: devoted to God
        (Luke 1:5-45)

what do you expect?

Think for a minute:

• How do you expect the God of heaven and earth to act?

The first chapter of Matthew refers to three names for God, all of which reveal some aspect of God's identity. Matthew 1:18 calls God "Jesus" and "Messiah," and verse 23 calls him "Emmanuel." *Jesus*, a common name of the time, meant "God saves." *Messiah*, a Hebrew word, means "savior." *Christ* is the Greek form of that name.

The Jews had been waiting for a messiah, a savior sent from God to deliver them from being ruled by foreign people who worshiped other gods—in this case, by the Romans. But the Jews expected a savior king who would come with power, brandishing a weapon and taking the world by storm. What they got was a savior king, who came with a different kind of authority. He spoke of peace, love, forgiveness, compassion, and being born of the spirit and water into a new creation. You can imagine how that message sounded to the waiting Jews.

In many ways, we still look for God to reveal God's self in flashy and majestic ways. Shouldn't the maker of heaven and earth be able to do some tricks and bring about world peace at the snap of some fingers? But we serve a God who gives freedom to make choices—to chose to live like Christ or like the kings of the world.

God has chosen to rely on us to work toward God's kingdom of peace. We do so by imitating the one who came as a compassionate servant seeking to care for the poor, the sick, the hungry, and the lonely. Ultimately, Jesus came so that we could have peace with God.

• What do you think about God choosing to come to earth as a compassionate servant?

Emmanuel!

Look up the passages below. Make notes about feelings Jesus must have experienced.

Mark 8:11-21:

John 2:13-16:

John 11:32-36:

John 12:37:

Mark 14:32-41:

John 18:2-5:

John 19:28:

John 19:1:

John 19:2-6:

John 20:24-25:

We worship a God who knows the depths of our feelings.

New Creation

new (noo) *adj.* 1. Not existing before; made or discovered for the first time. 2. Recently arrived. 3. Refreshed and restored. 4. Just beginning.

creation (kree-AY-shuhn) *n.* 1. The process of bringing something into existence. 2. Something that God has made.

For the love of Christ urges us on, because we are convinced that one has died for all; therefore all have died. And he died for all, so that those who live might live no longer for themselves, but for him who died and was raised for them.

From now on, therefore, we regard no one from a human point of view; even though we once knew Christ from a human point of view, we know him no longer in that way. So, if anyone is in Christ, there is a new creation; everything old has passed away; see, everything has become new!

—2 Corinthians 5:14-17 (NRSV)

Our firm decision is to work from this focused center: One man died for everyone. That puts everyone in the same boat. He included everyone in his death so that everyone could also be included in his life, a resurrection life, a far better life than people ever lived on their own.

Because of this decision we don't evaluate people by what they have or how they look. We looked at the Messiah that way once and got it all wrong, as you know. We certainly don't look at him that way anymore. Now we look inside, and what we see is that anyone united with the Messiah gets a fresh start, is created new. The old life is gone; a new life burgeons! Look at it!

—2 Corinthians 5:14-17 (*Message*)

A New Point of View

If not from a human point of view, from what other point of view can we regard others?

How do you change when when you look inside others? What do you do differently? Would others recognize Christ in your actions, attitudes, and words?

When have you judged others by their outward looks?
Or describe a time when you were ignored or made fun of.

How can you perhaps help someone else who is experiencing
those same things?

Who at school can you think of who needs someone to care
enough to help?

LIFE SONG

Which character in the video do you relate
to the most?

In what ways does your life song reflect
the new creation in you?

What are the things you do that
bring a smile to others?

44

A NEW CREATION IN CHRIST

We are called to be one with Christ, to be open with our hearts, our minds, and our souls. If we close off part of our lives by the choices we make or the attitudes we have, we separate ourselves from God. We must set aside those things that separate us from God, whatever they are, and let Christ live in us and through us.

How would having a fresh start in your life feel?

What might be keeping you from wanting to give yourself fully to God? Things that separate people from God include selfishness, focus on self, focus on money and material things, use of alcohol or other drugs, sexual activity, anger, impatience, envy, lack of self-control, jealousy, fear, apathy, greed, negative attitude, treatment of God's creation with disregard.

What are some of things that separate you from God? What do you need to give up to choose new-creation living?

What are some things you can do that will bring you closer to God?

Imagine what it would be like for you to live a resurrection life, to be a new creation in Christ. Are you willing to take the chance that your life could be even better than it has been?

Pray silently this prayer:

I don't know how to give you my all;
   but, Lord, I'm listening for you.
I don't know how to turn to you
      when it matters most;
   but, Lord, I'm trusting in you.
I don't know how to give up the old me;
   but, Lord, I want to be new in you.
I don't know how to get closer to you;
   but, Lord, I'm reaching for you.
Turn me to your ways.

                              Amen.

Peace

> **peace** (peess) *n.* 1. Freedom from quarrels or war. 2. Mental calm and serenity. 3. A handshake or kiss that people exchange during a service in some churches, symbolizing Christian love and unity.

"I'm telling you these things while I'm still living with you. The Friend, the Holy Spirit whom the Father will send at my request, will make everything plain to you. He will remind you of all the things I have told you. I'm leaving you well and whole. That's my parting gift to you. Peace. I don't leave you the way you're used to being left—feeling abandoned, bereft. So don't be upset. Don't be distraught."

—John 14:25-27 (*Message*)

List your first impressions after reading this passage.

What is happening in this story? Who is speaking? Who is listening?

Does the passage use the idea of peace as the opposite of war? What other words might describe the peace that is given here? Is the peace given a personal peace? peace to share in relationships with others? peace between nations?

(continued)

I've got peace like a river, I've got peace like a river;
I've got peace like a river in my soul.

—"I've Got Peace Like a River," spiritual

Do you think Jesus' peace is hard to find or difficult to recognize? Do you think it's harder for teenagers to find than for adults? What about children?

Why, do you think, did Jesus tell his disciples not to be afraid?

How does "well and whole" relate to peace?

What would be the opposite or an alternative to "feeling abandoned, bereft"?

How would you describe the kind of peace Jesus offers?

For God is a God not of disorder but of peace.

—1 Corinthians 14:33a

Breathing in Peace

WHAT PHRASE DID YOU USE FOR INHALING?

WHAT PHRASE DID YOU USE FOR EXHALING?

WHAT WAS YOUR EXPERIENCE LIKE WITH THIS KIND OF PRAYER?

I urge you to live a life worthy of the calling you have received. Be completely humble and gentle; be patient, bearing with one another in love. Make every effort to keep the unity of the Spirit through the bond of peace.

—Ephesians 4:1 b–3

And the peace of God, which surpasses all understanding, will guard your hearts and your minds in Christ Jesus.

—Philippians 4:7

LORD, MAKE ME AN INSTRUMENT OF YOUR PEACE.

—FROM THE "PRAYER OF ST. FRANCIS"

Psalm 91
A Psalm of Safety, Refuge, and Protection

You who live in the shelter of the Most High,
   who abide in the shadow of the Almighty,
will say to the LORD, "My refuge and my fortress;
   my God, in whom I trust."
For he will deliver you from the snare of the fowler
   and from the deadly pestilence;
he will cover you with his pinions,
   and under his wings you will find refuge;
   his faithfulness is a shield and buckler.
You will not fear the terror of the night,
   or the arrow that flies by day,
or the pestilence that stalks in darkness,
   or the destruction that wastes at noonday.
A thousand may fall at your side,
   ten thousand at your right hand,
   but it will not come near you.
You will only look with your eyes
   and see the punishment of the wicked.

Because you have made the LORD your refuge,
   the Most High your dwelling place,
no evil shall befall you,
   no scourge come near your tent.

For he will command his angels concerning you
   to guard you in all your ways.
On their hands they will bear you up,
   so that you will not dash your foot against a stone.
You will tread on the lion and the adder,
   the young lion and the serpent you will trample under foot.

Those who love me, I will deliver;
   I will protect those who know my name.
When they call to me, I will answer them;
   I will be with them in trouble,
   I will rescue them and honor them.
With long life I will satisfy them,
   and show them my salvation.

Guidance

guidance (GIGH-duhns) *n.* 1. The act of showing the way by advising, leading, or directing. 2. Information or advice aimed at resolving a difficulty, especially as given by an authority figure.

Jack's Story

Jack was home after school, exhausted from all the pressures he was facing. He had been trying to get everything done for classes, including ones he truly didn't care about, as well as deal with the relationship struggles he and his girlfriend always seemed to be having. To top off those problems, his dad had argued with him that morning about how irresponsible Jack supposedly was; Jack just tried not to think about that.

He dropped his backpack, grabbed some chips and soda, plopped down on the sofa, and started channel surfing. He was amazed at how he seemed to catch a commercial on every channel he flipped to. All the commericals seemed to be the same: "Just try this," "use this," "buy this," "vacation here and everything will be great!"

Jack found himself thinking, *Yeah? Well, you should try livin' my life, 'cause none of the products you're selling will change it for the better!* He started wondering where he might hear a more helpful message—one that could help him with all the things fighting for attention in his life.

GUIDANCE SYSTEM

What are some ways that can help you hear the signal of the Spirit of truth in the midst of all the noise in our world?

People hear God's message in various ways. How do you usually hear God's message for you? If you don't, what might you need to change to give God a chance?

What are things you can do on a regular basis to make yourself available to hear God's messages? Which will you focus on this week?

How will you put God's guidance into practice?

You are indeed my rock and my fortress;
> for your name's sake lead me and guide me
take me out of the net that is hidden for me,
> for you are my refuge.
Into your hand I commit my spirit;
> you have redeemed me, O LORD, faithful God.

> —Psalm 31:3-5

If you remove the yoke from among you,
> the pointing of the finger, the speaking of evil,
if you offer your food to the hungry
> and satisfy the needs of the afflicted,
then your light shall rise in the darkness
> and your gloom be like the noonday.
The LORD will guide you continually.

> —Isaiah 58:9b-11a

What clues do these two passages give
you about how we find God's guidance
in our busy, noisy world?

Second Coming

"Do not let your hearts be troubled. Believe in God, believe also in me. In my Father's house there are many dwelling places. If it were not so, would I have told you that I go to prepare a place for you? And if I go and prepare a place for you, I will come again and will take you to myself, so that where I am, there you may be also."

—John 14:1-3 (NRSV)

"Don't let this throw you. You trust God, don't you? Trust me. There is plenty of room for you in my Father's home. If that weren't so, would I have told you that I'm on my way to get a room ready for you? And if I'm on my way to get your room ready, I'll come back and get you so you can live where I live."

—John 14:1-3 (*Message*)

Jesus said to his disciples, "Don't be worried! Have faith in God and have faith in me. There are many rooms in my Father's house. I wouldn't tell you this, unless it was true. I am going there to prepare a place for each of you. After I have done this, I will come back and take you with me. Then we will be together."

—John 14:1-3 (CEV)

THE SECOND COMING

In the earliest days of Christianity, followers of Jesus believed that he would return in their lifetime. The "end of the age" was near. The hated Roman Empire would be destroyed, God's kingdom would come on earth, and all creation would be restored to the harmony once found in the garden of Eden. For this reason, Christians were consumed with the single goal of preparing spiritually.

When Jesus did not return as they had thought, they began to think in other ways. The Gospels were written so that the stories and teachings of Jesus could be kept alive. The Book of Revelation was written to offer hope to Christians suffering terrible persecution. The hope of a new tomorrow has continued through all of these generations.

The Gospel of Mark reminds us:

BUT ABOUT THAT DAY OR HOUR NO ONE KNOWS, NEITHER THE ANGELS IN HEAVEN, NOR THE SON, BUT ONLY THE FATHER. BEWARE, KEEP ALERT; FOR YOU DO NOT KNOW WHEN THE TIME WILL COME.

(Mark 13:32-33)

In the Meantime

If you type the term *Second Coming* into an Internet search engine, you'll find all kinds of wild stuff. Some people predict that Christ is coming right now or in the near future. They offer dire warnings of awful things about to happen.

These ideas are not new. Over the centuries, many people have tried to predict the time of the Second Coming. One prediction was that Jesus was coming again between 1843 and 1844. That foretelling came to be known as The Great Disappointment.

The Bible's main point is not to predict a day or a time. We don't know how long we are going to live. We all hope to live long and productive lives, but we know people who have died suddenly and sometimes tragically. One of the blessings of the Second Coming is the encouragement to live faithfully in the meantime.

The Bible reminds us to prepare ourselves by focusing our attention on how we live right now. How do we remain connected with God? How do we treat ourselves and our bodies? How do we behave toward the people we meet? How do we live in this brief period of time between our birth and our death, whenever that may be? How do we live faithfully so that *whenever* Christ comes again, we are ready?

Babysitting

Have you ever babysat for someone else's children? If you have, you know that babysitting can sometimes be a lot of fun and that it can also get pretty messy. Sometimes you know exactly what to do, and sometimes you wonder what you are doing there. Sometimes it is exciting; and when the kids don't want to go to bed, it can also get frustrating. Through it all, you know that you are taking care of the children until the parents come home.

In the space below, list at least six ways a babysitter carries out his or her responsibilities:

 1

 2

 3

 4

 5

 6

Claim the Life: Promise, Semester

We Christians are like babysitters. God is the parent. This earth and its people belong to God. Someday, God will reclaim all that is. Our responsibility is to take good care of this earth and its people—including ourselves—in the meantime. The task can be a lot of fun; it can be messy. We sometimes know exactly what to do; sometimes we get confused. We can be excited; we can be frustrated. But we know the parent will come again.

Look at your previous list. What clues do you find there for how you can be a babysitter for God's creation and God's people?

Promises, Promises

*For surely I know the plans
I have for you, says the LORD,
plans for your welfare
and not for harm,
to give you a future with hope.
Then when you call upon me
and pray to me,
I will hear you.*

—Jeremiah 29:11-12

Vows

> **vows** (vowz) *n.* 1. Solemn promises to perform a certain act or behave in a certain way. 2. A set of such promises committing one to a certain calling or role, such as confirmation or marriage.

Watch your step when you enter God's house. Enter to learn. That's far better than mindlessly offering a sacrifice, doing more harm than good.

Don't shoot off your mouth, or speak before you think. Don't be too quick to tell God what you think (God) wants to hear. God's in charge, not you—the less you speak, the better.

Over-work makes for restless sleep. Over-talk shows you up as a fool.

When you tell God you'll do something, do it—now. God takes no pleasure in foolish gabble. Vow it, then do it.

Far better not to vow in the first place than to vow and not pay up.

Don't let your mouth make a total sinner of you. When called to account, you won't get by with "Sorry, I didn't mean it." Why risk provoking God to angry retaliation?

But against all illusion and fantasy and empty talk. There's always this rock foundation: Fear God!

—Ecclesiastes 5:1-7 (*Message*)

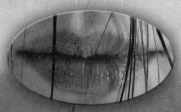

Claim the Life: Promise. Semester

PROMISES

"I'll stick with you."

"I'll clean up my room."

"I'll take care of you."

"I'll be faithful."

"I'll go to church."

"I'll always love you."

VOWS

"I'll follow Jesus."

"I'll clean up my life."

baptismal vows

confirmation vows

membership vows

marriage vows

VOWS TO GOD

"I accept Jesus Christ as my Savior."

"I promise to serve Christ as my Lord."

"I will remain a faithful member of Christ's holy church."

"I will nurture others in the faith and care for them as a part of Christ's family."

"I will support Christ's church with my prayers, presence, gifts, and service."

"With God's help, I will proclaim the good news and live according to the example of Jesus."

"I will by God's grace do everything in my power to uphold and care for these two persons in their marriage."

Promises, Promises

PROMISES THAT I'VE KEPT:

PROMISES THAT PEOPLE HAVE MADE TO ME AND KEPT:

PROMISES THAT I'VE BROKEN:

PROMISES THAT PEOPLE HAVE MADE TO ME AND THEN HAVE BROKEN:

Discipline

> **discipline** (DISS-uh-plin) *n.* 1. The training of people to obey a certain code of conduct, especially for moral improvement. 2. Controlled behavior resulting from such teaching.

MY REFLECTIONS

You have forgotten the exhortation that addresses you as children—

"My child, do not regard lightly
the discipline of the Lord,
or lose heart when you are punished by
[the Lord];
for the Lord disciplines those
whom [the Lord] loves,
and chastises every child whom [the
Lord] accepts.

Endure trials for the sake of discipline. God is treating you as children; for what child is there whom a parent does not discipline? If you do not have that discipline in which all children share, then you are illegitimate and not his children. Moreover, we had human parents to discipline us, and we respected them. Should we not be even more willing to be subject to the Father of spirits and live? For they disciplined us for a short time as seemed best to them, but [God] disciplines us for our good, in order that we may share [God's] holiness. Now, discipline always seems painful rather than pleasant at the time, but later it yields the peaceful fruit of righteousness to those who have been trained by it.

—Hebrews 12:5-11

What connections do you see between this Scripture and finding your way through the grid?

FROM HERE TO THERE

Together, write out directions to the two
places that your leader names.

First location:

Second location:

Which Way?

What was the difference between the two locations?

Which set of directions was more difficult to create? **Why?**

For the second location, which group's instructions would you follow if you really wanted to go there? **Why?**

I CHOOSE, I PROMISE

When you choose to be a student, you also promise to accept and even love the corrections of your teacher. If you want to learn something, you look forward to learning how to do it right. Finding out that you are off track can be frustrating in the moment; but when you look back on your mistake, you appreciate your teacher's insight that brought you back to the right path. You realize that if your teacher didn't care, he or she wouldn't have said anything. Discipline is a sign of love and compassion. It is offered by someone who cares about you and how you are living. He or she wants you to do right and live well.

Thanksgiving

thanksgiving (THANGKS-gih-veeng) *n.* An expression of gratitude or appreciation, especially to the Lord.

Rejoice always, pray without ceasing, give thanks in all circumstances; for this is the will of God in Christ Jesus for you.

—1 Thessalonians 5:16–18 (NRSV)

Be cheerful no matter what; pray all the time; thank God no matter what happens. This is the way God wants you who belong to Christ Jesus to live.

—1 Thessalonians 5:16–18 (*Message*)

An Attitude of Gratitude

Before I go to sleep at night, I try to name ten things I'm grateful for. It's easy to do; I can count off ten things by using my fingers. I like doing this little ritual. Sometimes I see how blessed I am, and sometimes I remember that things could be a lot worse.

—Matt McKennah, age 15

Sometimes I'm standing in the shower and the water feels so good. Then I start thinking about how good plain old water is; usually I just take it for granted. I start thanking God for being able to get clean, for feeling better after a shower than I did before, for getting to go swimming, and for having cool and clear water to drink whenever I want. Then I start thinking about places where not enough water is available or purified and people get sick a lot. That thought leads me to pray for those people. I remind myself that I have so much to be thankful for; I don't want to take the simple things for granted.

—Aisha Williams, age 17

One of the guys in my high school got killed last year in a crash. He was great guy. Pretty much everyone liked him. He was active in his youth group and was passionate about kids in Africa whose families were wiped out by AIDS. He'd done a couple of reports at school and an article for the school paper. When he died, we were just devastated. Then somebody started taking up money to send to one of the orphanages he had written about. Instead of us all feeling down, we had something we could do. I felt that we could sort of hang on to him and not let him be forgotten. I'm thankful that even though he died, his life will keep giving life.

—Dakota Langford, age 18

"In life, in death, in life beyond death, God is with us. We are not alone. Thanks be to God."

—"A New Creed,"
The United Church
of Canada

Test

test (tehst) *n.* A way of determining the worth, presence, quality, or truth of something.

gullible (GUH-luh-buhl) *adj.* Persuaded easily to believe something.

Do not quench the Spirit.
Do not despise the words of prophets,
but test everything;
hold fast to what is good;
abstain from every form of evil.

—1 Thessalonians 5:19-22 (NRSV)

Don't suppress the Spirit, and don't stifle those who have a word from the Master. On the other hand, don't be gullible. Check out everything, and keep only what's good. Throw out anything tainted with evil.

—1 Thessalonians 5:19-22 (Message)

KICK THE TIRES

You've been working after school and saving money wherever you could. Finally, you're car shopping!

You don't have a lot of cash, and you know you have to be careful not to overspend or you won't have money left for gas and insurance. So you're going to have to look for the right car. You can't afford repair bills!

The used-car salesman assures you this car is "the one." It looks great, but how will you know if it is great? What will you do? How will you test everything? Write your ideas anywhere on this page and the next page.

Test Standards

Hold On, or Let Go?

⬧ What are ways to test whether this thing is good or tainted with evil?

⬧ What from God's Word or from church teaching would be standards to apply?

⬧ Who could help us gain knowledge? Who could help us with discernment?

⬧ What or who might not be good help in this decision?

What Is Good?

Look up the Scriptures below, and write the standards that come from God's Word.

Matthew 22:37-39

Micah 6:8

What Is Evil?

John Wesley, the founder of the Methodist Movement, had three General Rules for living faithfully:

⋄ First, do no harm.

⋄ Second, do all the good that you can.

⋄ Third, attend to the ordinances of God (practices that bring us closer to God, such as worship, prayer, and service).

"<u>Do no harm</u>" is an easy-to-remember standard for identifying words and actions that are "tainted with evil."

Give some examples of things people do or say that are harmful to:

<u>Themselves</u>	<u>Others</u>	<u>God's Creation</u>

When you "test everything," what standards will you use?

Dance

dance (dans) *v.* To move in rhythm usually to music, using planned or improvised steps and gestures. *n.* A series of movements, usually matching the rhythm of a piece of music.

Never trust a spiritual leader who cannot dance.
—Mr. Miyagi
The Next Karate Kid (1994)

Nobody cares if you can't dance well. Just get up and dance.
—Dave Barry, humor columnist

You can dance anywhere, even if only in your heart.
—Anonymous

Dance is the only art of which we ourselves are the stuff of which it is made.
—Ted Shawn, choreographer

Dancing with the feet is one thing, but dancing with the heart is another.
—Anonymous

THE ARK OF THE COVENANT

God told Moses to build a tent, the tabernacle, for worship. Inside, in the area considered the Holy of Holies, was a special and ornate box. This Ark was sacred—it housed the stone tablets of the Ten Commandments, the sign of God's covenant with the people. The Ark of the Covenant symbolized God's presence with the people, first as they wandered in the wilderness and later in the Promised Land as the center of worship in the Temple.

THE EPHOD

The ephod, a garment similar to an apron, was worn over the clothes of high priests during specific rituals. Wearing the ephod was an important part of the ritual. When David danced wearing only an ephod, he acknowledged the importance of God over all else. David was declaring before everyone that this occasion was a supreme moment of worship and that nothing would come between him and worshiping God.

MICHAL

When David was a young man, the king at the time (Saul) felt threatened by David. So Saul came up with a subtle plan to do away with David. Knowing that his daughter Michal loved David, he promised her hand in marriage to David, provided he would bring proof that he had killed 100 Philistines, the enemies of the Israelites. Saul figured that David would neither succeed nor survive. However, David did; and Michal and David were wed.

Saul then plotted to have David killed. But Michal warned David, who escaped and went into hiding. With David gone, Saul gave Michal to another man. When Saul died, David had her sent back to him. Over time, David took several other wives, all of whom produced offspring for him; but Michal remained childless.

It is no wonder, then, that Michal found David's "dancing before the LORD" upsetting. Here was the man she had loved for years, the man whose life she had saved, dancing in total devotion to the God she perceived to have dealt her a raw deal in life—no children, no heirs, no value. What a terribly sad and bitter woman she must have been!

DANCING BEFORE GOD

Check out the Scriptures below. While each passage may not use the word *dance*, they all define how we can "dance before God." Jot down a note or two as you read the passages to remind yourself of how God wants us to worship.

Psalm 65:9 _____

Psalm 90:12 _____

Psalm 119:73 _____

Psalm 149:1 _____

Psalm 150:1 _____

Ecclesiastes 3:4 _____

Jeremiah 31:4 _____

Worshiping God should not be a fearful or embarrassing experience. It should not be a rating system where we sit in the back and judge the service based on a ten-point scale. It should not matter whether it "fits in" with other people's perceptions of worship. When you come into the presence of God, you enter holy ground; and that ground should become for you a place of joy and gratitude, a place that feels safe.

• Is there some way you would like to "dance before God" but wouldn't feel comfortable doing in your church?

• What is getting in the way of you dancing before God?

Promise

promise (PRAH-miss) v. To assure someone that one will do something or that something will happen. n. Such a statement or assurance.

Which of the promises in this study mean the most to you? Why?

What promises are you ready to make as a disciple of Jesus Christ?